CELEBRATE
JESUS

CELEBRATE LIFE

Leonard Edward Johnson

Published by:
Fortune Publishing Group
E-mail: info@fortunepublishinggroup.com
www.FortunePublishingGroup.com
Phone: (888) 910-6370

ISBN: 978-1-955358-21-7
Printed in the United States of America
Book cover designed by Max Fortune
Book edited by Joanna Johnson

Table of Contents

DEDICATION

This book is a testimonial. It is dedicated to anyone amid a storm, illness, or tragedy who finds themselves doubting the strength, ability and miracle working power of God in your situation. I am a living witness - God Can!!

Reverend William and Mrs. Bernice Johnson, Mom and Dad. Thank God for two loving parents who followed Jesus and loved the Lord. Mom prayed all day and night that God would keep me, even when I should not have been kept. Mom was a special lady. I dedicate this book to two parents who made a difference. I know they are watching over me. May they Rest in Peace.

ACKNOWLEDGMENTS

I pray that each word I use in the acronym CELEBRATE LIFE lifts you up and brings remembrance to all the reasons you must celebrate. I hope this message will cause you to reflect on how far you have come and you can celebrate with me for the joy in the journey.

I extend much love forever to my late Pastor, Rev. Dr. J.G. McCann, Sr., Mrs. McCann and the entire JGM ministry. I miss him deeply. I give honor to my Pastor, Rev. Dr. Shane Hilliard, a true believer in Christ, Church, Community, and Oneness. He is a truly anointed man of God assigned by God to be our Pastor of St. Luke Baptist Church in Harlem, New York. My deepest love and respect to my first cousin Joanna Chavis Johnson (JoJo). What a lady! I believe it is better to deserve honors and not have them than to have them and not deserve them. She deserves them all. She is very special to this family, and very special to me. True honors, JoJo. My oldest sister, Cynthia Johnson Jackson, is a tremendous blessing to me. She is the epitome of love. She speaks it, gives it, and seeks it with no limits. Her love is unconditional. Love looks through a telescope; it purifies and unlocks all doors. Her love opens doors. Love you, Big Sis. I must also acknowledge my sister, Lisa Johnson, aka ShowTime. I gave her that nickname. The Spirit is all in her DNA. I truly would not be the man I am without the love, support, and prayers of my siblings, Mary Ann, Patricia, Kim, and Antwon. I am thankful for them all. This family has so many powerful aunts, uncles, sisters, brothers, cousins, nieces, and nephews. I am thankful for them all.

I must also acknowledge my sons, Gary, Malcolm, and Marcus, and my daughters, Tamika, Chanelle, and Crystal. They are each special in their own way. I thank God for them. My wife, Alita N. Faircloth Johnson, is a woman who stayed with me through it all even though, at times, I did not deserve her unconditional love. I was a mess, but she was right there. She was right by my side through all my long, year-after-year hospital stays. That was a wife. Despite everything, I honor her as a good mother and friend. Our union has strengthened in the process, and I know that divided, we would fall. We stayed together in a way that should not happen – but God's plans are not our plans, and He is all in it.

I recognize all my St. Luke disciples. I have a love for them that will stay with me forever. I've been groomed for service under the tutelage, fellowship, leadership, and guidance of true soldiers of St. Luke. I love you all dearly.

To all my brothers I engage with on our phone line, you all know who you are. We dive in, and we keep it real about all subjects. Where would I be if I did not have strong brothers like you for life?

"As iron sharpens iron, so a friend sharpens a friend" (Proverbs 27:17).

Much love to Rev. Dennis, a true blessing in my life. Thank you. Ran, RD, Pee, and my big brother, Quas – Rest in heaven. Thanks to Mrs. Pollard, Kissie, KK, and Lamarr – blessings to the entire family.

I cannot call you all out, but trust that I am grateful for all the many friends and loved ones who have shared their lives, their stories, and their testimonies to enrich my life and strengthen my faith walk.

To my Brooklyn brothers that I grew up with – Reggie Henna, and Warren Heizel, we had some great times and created lots of memories that I will never forget. Blessings to you. I know that every day we face choices. I encourage you to trust God in all you do.

I met Dr. Peter Costantino in the emergency room at Mt. Sinai Hospital in 2006. I was laying in the emergency room in a lot of pain. Dr. Constantino was there checking on one of his patients and asked, "how can I help you". He found out what was happening with me from another physician on duty. He has been my main Dr. ever since. He is a great ENT physician who handled mostly all my tumor removal and associated surgeries. He took care of me like I was his brother. I extend undeniable love, respect and appreciation to him and I thank God every day for sending him my way. He stayed with me through it all and still checks on me to this day. I appreciate Dr. Costantino and wish God's richest blessing on him and his entire family.

Leonard Johnson and
Wife Alita Faircloth Johnson

Leonard Johnson, wife Alita & children: sons, Gary, Malcolm, Marcus, and my daughter, Tamika.

Cousin "Jo Jo" Joanna Johnson with Leanord Johnson

INTRODUCTION

Through over 15 surgeries to my head and face, and days and nights of excruciating pain, I kept praying and reading the Holy Bible as my strength and my guide. My steps were ordered, and God's plan for my life is still a work in progress. Even as soldiers for Christ, we are challenged by many storms in our lives. "Celebrate Jesus – Celebrate Life" will help you to understand that even when weary times come, you can find truth, strength, understanding, and peace in the word of God. God's word teaches us how to respond in all circumstances.

My late Pastor, Rev. Dr. J.G. McCann said, "It's not what happens to you, it's how you respond to it." I have found that the practice of celebrating life daily and consistently is the best way to respond to life challenges. It demonstrates our belief and reinforces our faith. It is confidence and assurance that God is in control of our life. Because of His almighty power, I know firsthand He is the God of a second chance.

My life is a miracle because God is a miracle worker. This devotional was borne out of my journey from brokenness to wholeness. "Celebrate Life" is the acronym through which my story is told. Each letter stands for an opportunity for worship and praise. Each letter in the two words of this title stands for the steps leading to an understanding of who God is and has been in my life. I discovered that to truly reap the benefits of God's amazing grace, I needed to make some changes. I had to **"Cash-in** "my ticket, **"Exit"** through the doors God closed behind me and enter the doors he opened, humble myself before

"*Leadership*," get "*Energized*," strengthen my "*Belief*," identify my "*Reasons*," or my purpose, take "*Action*," work "*Together*" with others for the glory of God, worship and feel the "*Excitement*" of the one who excites us most, Jesus. Then we can watch the blessings flow and the atmosphere change. I learned to "*Love*" again differently, to dance again with a different partner, refuel with "*Inspiration*" from God's word and rest in His enduring love for me. Today, I rely on my "*Faith*" to get me from day to day and will seek his face until the expected "*End*" – rejoicing all the way. I pray that my experiences will draw the reader into a deeper understanding of how sweet it is to be loved by God.

Leonard Johnson with Pastor Rev. Dr. J. G. McCann

CELEBRATE LIFE

When we celebrate life, it is a good time to look back over our life. It becomes clear that whenever our strength ran out, God's power began. I pray that reading this devotional will invigorate your faith and accelerate your belief in God's enduring love. Through my story, I hope you will understand how much turning your life over to God can be the best thing that ever happens to you. He will guide your footsteps and never leave you or forsake you – no matter what.

"For I know the plans I have for you," says the LORD. "They are plans for good and not for disaster, to give you a future and a hope." Jeremiah 29:11

Life can be long or short, but I have found that knowing our Savior and having a personal relationship with Him can give us joy along the journey. That joy shifts us to a higher plateau, ensuring that we still have a reason to celebrate no matter how long or short, or winding our path is. My life took some dangerous turns, but in the process, I learned that we cannot navigate this life alone. I discovered that I needed God. God is alive, and we know this because He is alive in us. When we speak this truth, we defeat the enemy by thwarting his plans and surrender ourselves to God's plan for us.

"Because you trusted me, I will give you your life as a reward. I will rescue you and keep you safe. I, the LORD, have spoken."
Jeremiah 39:18

I am a living, walking testimony that God has rewarded me with my life. Because of Him, I have no time to think negative thoughts. He came for me when I was not even seeking him. I remember where I was and where he brought me from. I went down, and he picked me up, took me in His arms, and rescued me. I will forever trust Him.

"If you cling to your life, you will lose it; if you give up your life for me, you will find it."
Matthew 10:39

I had my own plans for my life. I was hustling, making plenty of money. I did not think I needed anybody or anything. If I had stayed on that path, I could have ended up dead or in jail. I was raised in the church, my parents showed me the way, yet I was running in the opposite direction of God's plan for my life. When he came for me, I was lost, afraid, and sick, I had no choice but to humble myself before Him. I learned that you cannot hide from God. He sees all and knows all situations. When He controls your life, He can do the impossible. He has proved that time and time again in my life. He provides guidance, wisdom, and a new life. So, I will celebrate life every day, no matter what!!!!!

CASH – IN

"I know that you can do all things, no purpose can be thwarted". Job 42:2

I was born on Friday, July 26, 1957, at 1:36 a.m. at St. Johns Episcopal Hospital on Atlantic Avenue in Brooklyn, New York. That was the beginning of my journey. I was an early riser at birth and still get up early as an adult. I did not know it then, but God had a plan and purpose for my life. My Spirit was ready at birth, but my flesh had to learn to submit. So instead, I survived an extensive street life and an injury that eventually required multiple surgeries and long hospital stays that could have ended my life. God never left me. I did not know it, but my life was already bought.

"For you know that God paid a ransom to save you from the empty life, you inherited from your ancestors. And it was not paid with mere gold or silver, which lose their value." 1 Peter 1:18

I learned the hard way that Jesus paid the ultimate price for me when I was in my mother's womb. My price, my journey may be different from yours, but the sacrifice was for us all. The cost for my ticket might be higher than yours, but the good news is God already paid the price by sacrificing his only son on the cross for my redemption. All I had to do was Cash-In my ticket.

When Christ died on the cross, he paid a high price. He stood as our advocate, our lamb of God, and processed our tickets, yours, and mine. Our tickets were left at the Will-Call window waiting for us to pick them up. This ticket guarantees eternal life and freedom with our Lord and Savior, Jesus Christ. I finally picked up my ticket in 2001, cashed it in, and surrendered my whole life to Jesus Christ. I was baptized as an outward symbol of my internal conversion. I was washed clean, redeemed, and given an opportunity for a second chance. The Bible declares that...

"As far as the east is from the west, our transgressions have been removed from us." Psalms 103:12

I identified with Jesus' death, his burial, and his resurrection. Old sins were washed away, and I took on a new way of life in Christ Jesus. When I was dipped in that water, I came up clean. I CASHED-IN, placed my life in the will of God. My life changed to fulfill his purpose, my confidence changed, and my faith increased, but it didn't get easy after I cashed in.

In 1990, I was diagnosed with meningioma. A meningioma is a tumor arising from the meninges — the membranes surrounding the brain and spinal cord. Although not technically a brain tumor, it is included in this category because it may compress or squeeze the adjacent brain, nerves, and vessels. Meningioma is the most common type of tumor that forms in the head. Treatment required multiple surgeries, radiation, and different deadly antibiotics were administered to save my life. However, ultimately, God renewed my strength minute by minute, day by day, and I'm still here to tell my story.

"He renews my strength. He guides me along right paths, bringing honor to his name." Psalms 23:3

4

I am reminded of the words in Gladys Knight's song, "If anyone should ever write my life story, for whatever reason there might be," Between all the pain and the rough times – God is the best thing that ever happened to me. He will always be there, and I am so glad I "cashed-in" when I did. Glory Hallelujah!

EXIT

I love "old-school" R&B music. Teddy Pendergrass sang songs that gave you that get-up-and-dance vibe in your body. The words of some of his songs evoked emotion but also deliverance. Remember, "Wake up everybody, no more sleeping in bed... no more backward thinking, time for thinking ahead," "You Can't Hide from Yourself," "Tell the World," "How I Feel About You, Baby." Deciding to walk with God requires leaving some things, some people, some thoughts, some habits, and some behaviors behind. It is a difficult decision to make as we do not always know how and when to exit or where we are entering.

God is always knocking at our door, reaching into our hearts and soul. The question is, will we answer the door? He is always available. I encourage you to wake up, look in the mirror, and have a heart-to-heart with Jesus. He is at the door of your decisions, and you can always reach Him in prayer.

"And when you pray, do not be like the hypocrites, for they love to pray to stand in the synagogues and on the street corners to be seen by others... But when you pray, go into your room, close the door, and pray to your Father, who is unseen. Then your Father, who sees what is done in secret, will reward you...your Father

> ### *knows what you need before you ask him."*
> ### *Matthew 6:5-8*

You will discover that He provides the exit and is waiting at the entrance with open arms to receive you. Most times, a quiet, special moment with God is all we need. My illness left me flat on my back, racked in pain, and alone. I did not share what was happening to me with my siblings right away. I rarely had visitors. In those silent moments, I learned to depend on God and trust that He is the only way to both our exits and our entrances.

I remember a sermon by the late Pastor, Dr. Shellie Sampson, entitled "Thinking about What You're Thinking About." Think about the doors that have closed behind you and those that have been opened for you. Reflect on those things, and let those recollections guide your future decisions. What and who have you left behind as you move about in your career, while driving in your car, as you walk into your church? What challenges have you avoided? What unbelievable opportunities have you missed? Are you walking in God's favor with confidence or questioning your every step? What is your plan?

> ### *"Commit thy works unto the Lord and thy*
> ### *thoughts shall be established."*
> ### *Proverbs 16:3*

We all have access to the promise of "hope and a future" by answering the knock and exiting a life without God. To exit the laws of our flesh, we must believe that the Savior is real and that His exit was a sacrifice for us. His exit took three days, but he returned with all power in his hands. Our sacrifice is simply saying Yes to His will and walking into the life He has prepared for us. We will still be tested, as I am every day. He continues to strengthen my mind and my body. I thought I knew the right exit until I learned that...

> ### *"The heart of man plans his way, but the Lord*
> ### *establishes his steps."*
> ### *Proverbs 16:9*

Pastor, Rev. Dr. J.G. McCann, Sr., referred to the acronym BIBLE as "Basic Instructions Before Leaving Earth." I challenge everyone to get this instruction. Wake up, no more sleeping in bed. You cannot hide from yourself. If you do not have a relationship with Jesus, please consider it. God has a customized exit plan for you. I encourage you to say Yes to His will.

"Enter through the narrow gate. For wide is the gate, and broad is the way that leads to destruction, and there are many who go in by it. But small is the gate, and difficult is the way which leads to life, and only a few will find it." Matthew 7:13,14

LEADERSHIP

I had the privilege of knowing a true leader. The man was a trendsetter with a foundation of honesty, exemplary character, integrity, faith, love, balance, and loyalty to Jesus. I heard him preach when I first came across Rev. Dr. J.G. McCann, Sr., in 1999-2000. My first impression was, wow, who is this man of God? I thought this preacher must be an advocate associated with the human rights leaders of the country. He must be running for political office. I compared him to leaders like Malcolm X, Martin Luther King, Adam Clayton Powell, "Keep hope alive," Jessie Jackson, and Rev. Al Sharpton, the people's preacher.

I thought to myself, this man can make a difference. His messages moved me deeply. I wanted to know who this man was. So, I decided to go up to the alter and become a disciple of this ministry. For a short time I had become a Muslim, and for even a shorter time I became a Mason, but I was not pleased. When I connected with Rev. McCann, I felt I had connected with a real leader. This was leadership that helped me to get a closer connection with our Lord and Savior, Jesus Christ. He became my spiritual advisor, Pastor, and mentor. He had a special walk, talk, and message that seemed to get all up in your situation. His messages would touch your heart and your mind. It kept me coming back. He was a great leader who would not lead you astray. He helped me to stay grounded in church, which was something I never thought I would do. I found myself happy in Jesus' protected arms.

In one of Rev. McCann's sermons, he preached from Exodus 14-15:

And the Lord said to Moses, why do you cry to me? Tell the children of Israel to go forward.

That is the strength of leadership. The questions he posed to us were: Are you, the people of Egypt – stuck in one place? Are you the wilderness people going around and around in circles? Or are you promised land people trusting our Savior Jesus Christ? I reflected on those questions and decided that with faith in God, I would follow a true leader with a vision and desire to pull us all out of the pit and help us live a victorious life. I choose to trust Jesus Christ. I stepped up, followed my Pastor, and became wholly involved in the ministry of the gospel. One of Rev. McCann's many messages to the people of faith that still speaks to me today was called, "Forward Forever, Backwards Never ." That is now my mantra.

Rev. McCann became my mentor and my friend. I truly miss my Pastor. He made a difference. His Spirit and his leadership live on, and I will honor his legacy by sharing God's goodness in my life with others and following the standards of leadership example that he set.

"Do nothing out of selfish ambition or vain conceit. Rather, in humility, valuing others above yourselves, not looking to your own interests but each of you to the interests of the others. In your relationships with one another, have the same mindset as Christ Jesus: Who, being in very nature, God did not consider equality with God something to be used to his own advantage; rather, he made himself nothing by taking the very nature of a servant, being made in human likeness."
Philippians 2:3-7

ENERGY

It is God that girds me with strength, and makes my way perfect (Psalm 18:32)

Sometimes we wake up in the morning without energy or just feeling sluggish or overwhelmed by different life responsibilities. In those times, who or what can energize you? Where are you getting your daily dose of energy from? Most of us know what lies ahead of us and our schedule for the day, so we take the necessary steps to get moving. I fall on my knees, sometimes in tears, and just rest in God's presence. In that space, I give God all the praise, glory, and honor, calling his name, Jesus, Jesus, Jesus, and thanking him for letting me wake up again. Despite my circumstances, I am awake, I am grateful, and I am energized. A new energy, a new day with new mercies ahead.

When I was going through my sickness, two words settled deep in my mind and in my heart. Staying alive was a rough encounter. I looked around and at myself, and I cried out loud to myself repeatedly every day and every night while lying in the hospital wrapped up in pads, and bandages around my head, swollen bloodlines, draining tubes with blood bags coming out of my surgery area, connected to lines of medication, breathing tubes, and heart regulators. I was pretty messed up. The tumor went six inches to my brain. They had to freeze my head to bring down the swelling. Each day I had to wrestle with the pain. I had to see myself out of this situation, not knowing if

I would ever be back again. I told myself to stop crying and worrying about things I could not control and to celebrate life instead. I was still alive. I could still celebrate the greatness and the awesomeness of God's power. God's love was unquestionable, even at that moment. I was still alive to tell my story.

Issues will come, but there is an app for that. It's called the Armor of God:

"Finally, be strong in the Lord and his mighty power. Put on the full armor of God so that you can take your stand against the devil's schemes. Our struggle is not against flesh and blood but against the rulers, the authorities, the powers of this dark world, and the spiritual forces of evil in the heavenly realms. Therefore, put on the full armor of God so that when the day of evil comes, you may be able to stand your ground and, after you have done everything, stand. Stand firm then, with the belt of truth buckled around your waist, the breastplate of righteousness in place, and your feet fitted with the readiness that comes from the gospel of peace. In addition to all this, take up the shield of faith, with which you can extinguish all the flaming arrows of the evil one. Take the helmet of salvation and the sword of the Spirit, which is the word of God."
Ephesians 6:10-17

Pastor McCann used to say, "We plan, God laughs ." Find joy where you can. Another McCann acronym was JOY (Jesus first, Others second, Yourself last). Wake up celebrating life to get that spiritual power boost early in the morning. Pray throughout the day as you walk, think, and plan. God will send a refreshing and give you all the energy you need.

Dr. McCann had so much energy. He energized me. Up early - Down late. One assignment after another. If you live a busy life, you need God's energy. On a bad day, he was energized and shared that energy with those around him. I followed his lead. Think positive and be faithful. Call on Jesus immediately as your eyes open in the morning. Thank God that you are alive to make a greater impact for God through your life. It's a new day...new energy awaits you. Look Up and Live! For the word of God is living and active and full of power (making it operative, energizing and effective). Hebrews 4:12

BELIEVE

"Wisdom is the principal thing, therefore get wisdom and in all your getting, get understanding." Proverbs 4:7

According to Webster, faith is a strong belief in God or the doctrines or teachings of religion. The Bible declares that faith is the assurance of things hoped for and the conviction of things not seen. When I can look at a chair and see that all the legs are sturdy, the back is strong, and the frame is large enough to fit my body, I have faith that the chair will not drop me to the floor. I have faith that when I go to the airport, the plane that I board will get me to my desired destination. We all exercise a little bit of faith every day. We assume that when we leave our house every day to go to work, we will return at the expected time. So, sometimes we take our faith for granted.

I knew that if I was going to survive, I had to elevate my faith walk. I had to increase my confidence in the word, the Holy Bible, and the gospel that my Pastor preached about, and my faith in God had to grow to a higher level. I had to learn that faith is not a casual exercise that randomly falls on us, but enduring faith and empowering faith requires work.

One of my many surgeries lasted 7 hours; then, they had to go back in for another 6 hours. In each surgery, the doctor had to take a part of my body- a chest muscle, a leg muscle, and three different skin grafts on my lower right leg fibular bone. Once each body part is altered, your natural ability to move is hindered. It affects your blood flow because your body must adjust to your new frame. It's a slow process. It is an even greater effort to return to a normal way of moving and being strong again. I was a boxer. I was accustomed to being physically fit, agile, and strong, yet here I was, too weak to move. I had every reason to lose hope so many times, but God said, "Not Yet," and I believed Him.

My foundation was strong. My faith was reinforced by studying the word of God regularly and maintaining my faith, even in bad times. I found that if you believe in the word of God and immerse your daily activities and situations in the promises and instructions of God, you will see his power manifested in everything you do. If you surround yourself with positive people who believe and pour into your life, it helps build your belief tremendously.

Again, I credit my Pastor, a real leader with scriptural knowledge and Bible beliefs rooted in Jesus Christ, who taught us that we will be alright. If our faith is rooted in Jesus Christ, like the Sequoia tree roots are in the ground, our faith cannot be moved. Build up your faith. Believe you can achieve, believe it can be done. Believe you will accomplish the dream and the thoughts you spoke to God and yourself about.

If you really want to eat a great meal, start reading at Genesis and read through to Revelations. Read and study all 66 books (39 in the Old Testament and 27 in the New Testament). Pastor McCann used to say, while you are reading, beginning at Genesis - the meat, throw away the bone. I have come to the realization that the Word of God is truly a "lamp unto my feet, and a light unto my path (Psalms 119:105). It is my belief guide and navigator to recovery. Try it, and never, ever think twice about what God can do. Believe that.

"He that believeth on me, as the scripture hath said, out of his belly shall flow rivers of living water. (John 7:38)

REASONS

"Abundant peace belongs to those who love Your instruction; nothing can make them stumble."
Psalms 119:165

Reason - a statement presented in justification or explanation of a belief or action. It is important to understand why things happen and how I can still justify that Jesus Christ is real in my life. It is important to understand that the love I have is not just a fleeting emotion brought on from being caught up in a moment or enticed by a temporary high. Unlike the song titled "Reasons" by the very popular R & B group, Earth, Wind, and Fire, "All our reasons will never start to fade." It is more than a one-night fantasy. The reasons why we are here, the reasons why our feelings for Jesus Christ will never disappear, are revealed in the life we live and the battles we have overcome.

My love for soul music did not disappear when I gave my life to Christ. As I stated previously, I still love music, and I still love to dance. I just dance with a different partner now. I still recall and reflect upon the music of my upbringing. Back in those days, we had some of the greatest artists who sang songs that would lift your soul to another level. I remember greats like Marvin Gaye, Gladys Knight, The Temptations, the O'Jays, and so many others. Those songs remind me of periods in my life when the lyrics were relevant to what was going on in the world. For example, the Temptations sang, "People moving in, people moving out because of the color of their skin...run, run, run, but you sure can't hide." The events of our past and the decisions we made are all a result of our exposure and our environment. I believe that just as artists sang songs of the times that take us back, we must also tell our stories of our struggles, our battles – the good and the bad, because therein lies our testimony. And sharing our testimonies is one of the reasons we are here.

I found that my reason, my overcoming story was personal, and honestly, I was hesitant to share it. I can only speak for myself, but 19 surgeries in 25 years, not including the one I had back in the 70s, was not just your average test. In the 70s, I was diagnosed with meningitis at the Joint Disease Hospital in Harlem on Madison Avenue. I remember it like it was yesterday. God had a reason.

When something tragic happens, people say, "Why me?' My response to that is, "Why Not You?" You have heard the expression, "Your test is your testimony." I believe that, in my case, that is true. I must tell my story!

I was in the intensive care unit (ICU) 5 times, each time for 7, 8, or 9 days. Each stay was different. ICU is the last chance to make it after a major surgery. They watch you all day and all night, fixing and changing things. When you get better, they take you to the second level. It is called the surgical step-down unit. Here, they administer different intravenous medications that help you get to a regular room. Every step of the way, God said, "Not Yet" "Let's Go," "Be in it to Win it," and "Stay Focused ." "Follow your goals in life". Encouraged by the word, I listened.

"Since you have been raised to new life with Christ, set your sights on the realities of heaven, where Christ sits in the place of honor at God's right hand. Think about the things of heaven, not the things of earth. For you died to this life, and your real life is hidden with Christ in God,

and when Christ, who is your life, is revealed to the whole world, you will share in all his glory."
Colossians 3:1-4

We all have a reason, a testimony to be shared, to lift others, to talk about the goodness of our Lord and Savior. Some setbacks are a setup for a comeback. I found with God in your life, all things are possible. Just look up and say, thank you, Lord, for giving me another chance. Giving my life to Jesus was a reasonable choice. He pulled me up out of the pit, from pain to power!! It was God's Holy Ghost power that spared me to tell my story. That's my reason. What is yours?

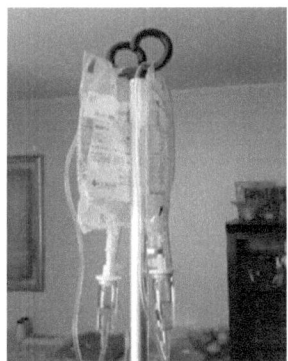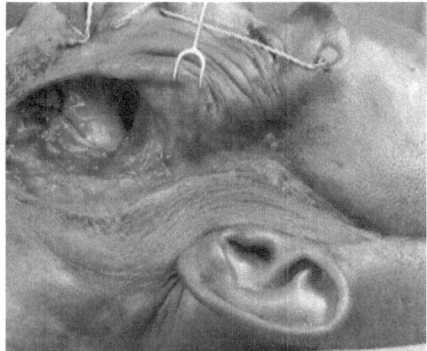

The Surgeries Begin...

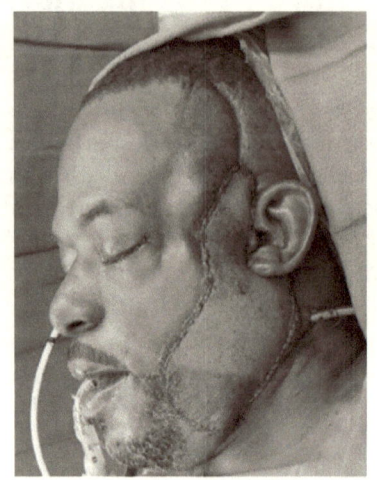 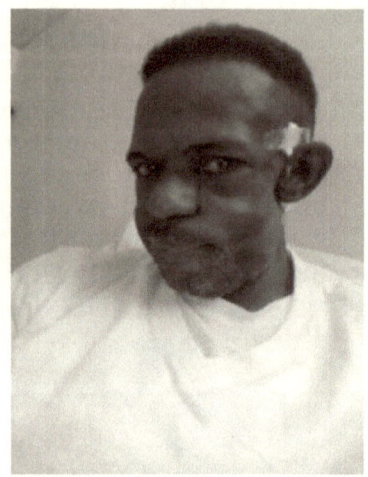

And Successfully Ends

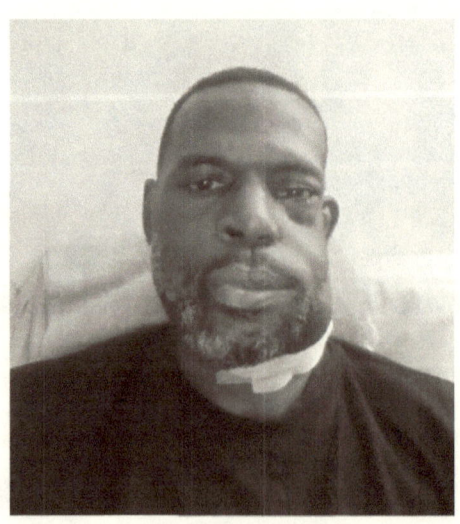

ACTION

Webster defines action as "the accomplishment of a thing usually over a period of time, in stages, or with the possibility of repetition ." Action represents consistency – like a well-oiled machine, and we rely on it to run smoothly once it is programmed and set. As a child of God, we are challenged to live a life of action, consistently representing the power within us. The Holy Spirit is the power within us. The Spirit, like the word ACTION, is sometimes loud; it is strong, it moves things, and it moves us.

The Spirit is like the wind, it moves things also. We cannot see it, but we can see its effects. The wind causes the leaves to rustle at the tops of trees or causes dry leaves to swirl in midair. We can feel a gentle breeze from the ocean on our faces. The wind is also strong; it can cause a 200,000-ton cruise ship to sway on the sea. The wind, like action, is powerful. It can tear down a building or wipe out a whole community caught up in an angry tornado. Our actions are our works, and our works yield power. That power is a demonstration of the Holy Spirit.

In my most trying moments, I used action to invoke the Holy Spirit into my circumstance. I cried out loud to the Lord many times. When I lost my speech and my ability to swallow, I praised God and gave him all the glory and honor on the inside. Every day I wake up, I begin my day in fervent prayer, worship, praise, dance, and throw my hands in the air. Today, I have my voice, I can speak again. That's action, and because of that, I celebrate life daily.

Our greatest mistake is when we don't commit to activating our faith through action in our walk, talk, thoughts, and behaviors. We don't get things done because, instead, we procrastinate. It takes action to pursue happiness, integrity and to achieve our dreams. Things happen when we discipline ourselves to vocally call on the name of Jesus, our motivator, our Savior. For every disciplined effort, there is a multiplied reward, and action always flows with something behind it. Fear not, no matter the situation – act, and watch God change things.

"As the body without the Spirit is dead, so faith without deeds is dead."
James 2:26

"For everything that was written in the past was written to teach us, so that through the endurance taught in the Scriptures and the encouragement they provide, we might have hope."
Romans 15:4

TOGETHERNESS

The Bible teaches us in **Matthew 18:20** that "**Where two or three gather together in my name, there am I with them.**" The concept of togetherness or unity is a consistent theme throughout the Bible. In Zephaniah, brothers are encouraged to come together, bringing their unique and individual gifts to build each other up (Zephaniah 2:1). In I Corinthians, brothers are implored to speak the same thing, that there be no divisions, and that...

"You be perfected together in the same mind and in the same judgement." I Corinthians 1:10

It took me years to understand how powerful and how impactful building and keeping a strong united brotherhood would be in my life, personally and corporately.

My Pastor, Rev. Dr. Shane Hilliard, speaks of "Oneness" and how together, we can accomplish so much...but we have issues. It is a cliché in the black community, based on the traumas of separation in our past and societal mechanisms designed to separate us that "we cannot work together," that "we are like crabs in a barrel." Everyone says they are willing to work together, so they say, but not always able. In my experience, there seems to always be baggage blocking our progress. Sometimes, we are guilty of bringing baggage with us, but ultimately, we are not meant to travel through this life alone. We all need each other. As Christians, the Word instructs us to work together. Pastor McCann Sr. used to say, "We all need a ride-or-die friend. We need someone who will not bail out on us. We need someone who will be an encourager to keep us together." There is an inherent power when we gather in Spirit and in the name of our Lord, Jesus Christ. The Psalms speak of **how good and pleasant it is when God's people live together in unity. (Psalms 133:1)**

My late Pastor, Rev. J.G McCann, believed in building a community of faith. He had a vision for the church. So, when all the St. Luke disciples, including myself, joined together in oneness with the same beliefs and goals, his vision ultimately came to fruition. This was a living example of how the Spirit of God indwells us collectively. We unite around a common cause that pleases our Father. Our unique gifts of the Spirit collaborate to carry out that which God has set out for us to do. Essentially, we become a functioning and effective body of Christ. The work of this church affects the whole community, and everyone benefits.

When Pastor Rev. Hilliard picked up the mantel, he carried on the vision, preached the same philosophy of Christ, Church, and Community, and instructed us that this is what togetherness looks like. He further recommended that we should never try to bloom before our time but that we intentionally grow together and look out for one another. This lesson was personal for me.

Having a brotherhood of faith, praying together, sharing our experiences and our mess ups, looking out for each other, and lifting each other up has strengthened my resolve and belief that my disability was not the end for me. Instead, it was the beginning of getting back on track, restoring my hope and trust in God. In many ways, I learned that my disability was not just physical but mental. Our group intentionally worked to renew our minds and live our lives, believing it is not what happens to us but how we respond to it. Don't underestimate the power of Christian unity.

A New Life – Leonard with Fellow Deacons

EXCITEMENT

Jesus brings us so much excitement. When the power of the Holy Spirit fills a room, praise and worship break out, and the atmosphere changes. People are shouting, running, and dancing in the Spirit. The old folks used to say, "It's like fire shut up in my bones." It is a feeling I had never experienced before, but when I did, I could not help but compare it to a good house party.

I love to dance, and I love good R&B music. Good music with a good beat sends a special groove through my body. My legs and arms get to moving, my fingers popping, my hands clapping – I can't keep still, and I'm moving from side to side. I consider a good party with good music and lots of dancing the ultimate excitement.

When I got saved, I thought that excitement about music and dancing was over, but I discovered I was dead wrong. It never ended. Those Holy Ghost filled spiritual songs move me just the same. When I check into this house of "excitement," the house of worship, and when high praises go up in music and songs, the Spirit begins to move me. Except now, I am dead to the flesh and wrapped up in a holy, hallelujah one on one connection with the Lord. I found out that my worship is personal, and the mixture of the Word and the atmosphere of praise gets caught up in my bones. I can holler, jump, and dance in my own way. Those shouters really know how to get busy. I am not a shouter, but I am happy to be in His presence, connected to the most exciting and uplifting, Jesus Christ. When I call out his name, I praise him for his sacrifice at the cross for me, and I cannot help but worship him like it's just me and Him.

If you want to experience joy, real excitement, and get motivated - try Jesus. If you want to get the boost you have been missing, begin to worship the Lord with all your heart and soul and let the Holy Spirit, through the songs of praise, usher you into his presence. Dance for Jesus, the greatest creator of real uplifting excitement, and watch the atmosphere change.

Praise the Lord

Praise God in His sanctuary; praise Him in his mighty heavens.

Praise Him for His acts of power; praise Him for His surpassing greatness.

Praise Him with the sounding of the trumpet, praise Him with the harp and lyre,

Praise Him with timbrel and dancing...

Let everything that has breath praise the Lord.

Psalms 150:1-6

LOVE

"Love the Lord your God with all your heart and with all your soul and with all your strength and with all your mind; and Love your neighbor as yourself." Jesus replied, "Do this, and you will live."
Luke 10:27-28

I was blessed to see this type of love in my mother at an early age. She loved the Lord, and she loved cooking and making different dishes for me, my siblings, and my neighbors in the hood. She was loved very much because of that. Everyone loved Mrs. Bernice Johnson for her cooking. Although we didn't have much, she shared love by giving other families some food. Thank God my father brought home the cash. It wasn't much, but just enough. That's love. Although she was a perfect example of the love of God, I had to learn love for myself.

As babies, we had no special love. We just wanted to see our mommy, get a bottle when we were hungry and always see the same faces. As I got older, love became a sort of mystery. I know that the word "love" can be an action verb. Love can also mean an attachment to someone for life. Love can also be a noun, a person, place, or thing that makes you feel warm inside. Love is a tender word or touch. Love is sexual. Yes, indeed, we all learn something about love in those moments. Consider these definitions and ask yourself how you experience and define love. Who do you love? What do you love? Can you remember why you fell in love? Are you loved back? We come across all different kinds of love on this life journey.

But when I decided to give my life to Christ, I found the greatest love of all, real love. God's love is different from anything I have experienced. When you fall in love with Jesus, it's forever. He will never let you go. It's a feeling deep in your soul. Jesus' love is so affectionate. It brings loving tears to your eyes. You can't help but look up, raise your hands, and praise Him. God's love is eternal. He sacrificed his blood on the cross, paid the price for us, and promised to love us forever. If He loves us that much, the least we can do is honor Him by loving and caring for others, with no reservations, making it a regular or natural part of our daily lives. Keep praying, and keep loving just as Christ loves us. Follow the word and trust that God's love is forever.

"If I speak in the tongues of men or of angels, but do not have love, I am only a resounding gong or a clanging cymbal."
I Corinthians 13-1

He answered,

"Love the Lord your God with all your heart and with all your soul and with all your strength and with all your mind; and love your neighbor as yourself." ***Luke 10:27,28***

"Above all, love each other deeply because love covers over a multitude of sins."
I Peter 4:8

Leonard Johnson with Siblings

INSPIRATION

Tell me, beloved, what inspires you? Who inspires you when they show up, or you hear from them? Is there anyone in your life who inspires you? Well, there are many who inspire you in so many ways. Your son, your daughter, aunt, uncle, cousin? These people around you may have the potential to give you that inspirational energy to help you keep going forward in life.

We have issues that cause us to need inspiration from others. Cancer, loss of a limb, and major health issues that did not look good are times when one might benefit from inspiration from others. You may need someone to inspire you to look up, get up, and keep going.

The most inspired moment in my life was giving my life to Jesus. That gave me energy, and that feeling has never left me. Each moment I was on my back, I looked up towards heaven, smiled, and said, "Lord, God, I am in your hands . I'll see you on the other side." Every time I woke up from one of those 19 surgeries, I just said, "Thank you, Jesus, thank you, Jesus." God is my inspiration, and going through that was the most inspirational time of my life. Having a close relationship with God, the mighty inspirer is all we will ever need.

I encourage you to reach out to a loved one you have not spoken to or seen in a while. Reach out to a friend that you know may be going through something. Give them an inspiring word; speak over their life in Jesus' name. Rev. Dr. J.G. McCann, Sr. inspired me to live in a Godly and inspiring way. What an extraordinary inspiration he was for me! I thank God for him.

"Is anyone among you in trouble? Let them pray. Is anyone happy? Let them sing songs of praise"
James 5:13) "And the prayer offered in faith will make the sick person well; the Lord will raise them up. If they have sinned, they will be forgiven."
James 5:15

FAITH

F aith alone cannot save you, but if you have faith in Jesus Christ, your soul is covered. A little faith will bring your soul to heaven, but a lot of faith will bring heaven to your soul. I am convinced that the lack of faith in God is the source of society's troubles.

"Faith is the substance of things hoped for and the evidence of things not seen." Hebrews 11:1

That means that we can have assurance and confirmation that what we hope for can be divinely guaranteed if we trust in God. My late great Pastor, Rev. Dr. McCann, Sr., taught us about the 20 Articles of Faith: Faith (Exodus 24:4), True God (Genesis 1:1), The Fall of Man (Genesis 1:26-30), God's Purpose of Grace (Ephesians 1:3, 13), The Way of Salvation (Ephesians 2:8-10), Generation (John 3:3), Repentance (Matthew 4:17), God of Faith (Romans 5:12), God of Justification (Romans 5:17,21), God of Adoption (Peter 2:9-10), God of Sanctification (Hebrews 2:3), The Perseverance of the Saints (Ephesians 1:13-14), The Law of the Gospel (Acts 15:11), A Gospel Church (Matthew 1:18-19), Christian Baptism (Matthew 3:16), the Lord's Supper (Matthew 26:26,28), The Christian Sabbath (Acts 20:7), Civil Government (Matthew 22:21), Righteousness and the Wicked (Revelation 20:10; 22:5), The World to Come (Titus 2:12,13). The study of these articles helped me build an armor, a shield of protection around my life and actions, strengthened my walk with Christ, and showed me the power of knowledge. When life throws fiery darts and arrows my way, whenever I am discouraged or lose my way, I go back to the Word of God and peruse the Articles of

Faith laid out for us. I learned, in a very personal way, that everything we need, the answers to complex problems, direction when there is a fork in the road, peace when there is a storm, and comfort when there is sorrow, can be found in the pages of the Holy Word, outlined strategically throughout these articles of faith. I encourage you to open the book for yourself. Do not be faithless. He who is small in faith is small in Christ. Your faith will lead you to greatness.

> *"Now unto him who is able to do far more abundantly than all that we ask or think, according to the power at work within us, to him be glory in the church and in Christ Jesus throughout all generations. forever and ever. Amen"*
> *Ephesians 3:20*

We all must find a confidant, someone, or something to trust in. I choose to trust in God! Trust shows your faith. Strong faith covers all areas of your life. Healing is covered by faith; relationships are covered by faith. Safety is covered by faith. We all struggle with something at different times, in different ways. Still, I know that when storms come– our faith helps us to move forward – to get up with strength and determination; because of our faith in the true and living God, we can keep moving. Just look at me!!!

> *"And the prayer offered in faith will make the sick person well; the Lord will raise them up. If they have sinned, they will be forgiven."*
> *James 5:15*

END
(My Testimony)

It's over. I have reached my limit. I felt that I had come to the full extent of my life, and my journey was over. I questioned, is this the end? But I discovered that what I thought was the end was a new beginning. As I lay in that sick room, I cursed myself. "I should have stopped, I should have made that turn; I should have listened; I was told the truth, but I did not listen." I am sure you have been there.

I did things my way most of my life. My life took a turn for the worst; it started changing right before my eyes. I was caught up in a dangerous and unnecessary lifestyle. When a view of my life coming to an end was apparent or appeared to be getting closer, so I thought, I pondered on these things. But it was not too late to turn. There is still time to learn. I had to earnestly seek wisdom and understanding for myself. No one could save me.

I had to seek Godly wisdom, get understanding by actively seeking spiritual discernment, mature comprehension, and logical interpretation, then apply it daily to my life. There was no other way. One of my favorite sayings comes from Pastor McCann's book, *"31 Days, 31 Keys to the Kingdom."*

"There are many things in the Bible I cannot understand. I only think I understand, but there are many things I cannot misunderstand."

This was a direct message to me, my wake-up call to truly seek wisdom concerning my life.

I woke up and gave my life to Christ. I realized after all that I had been through, and it was so much; if I wanted to make it to the end in a good way – something had to change. I had another chance to get it right. I had the opportunity to forget about all the bad days and obstacles that could have blocked me from getting to the gate.

I wanted to enter God's gate at the end. I wanted to see my mother and Father and my loved ones again. I knew that I would be headed to Hell if I did not change my direction. And God was gracious; He left me here to tell you about Him.

Let this story encourage you. Open your eyes. Visualize the best thing you could ever be a part of. Sit in the presence of our Savior, you know Him, the Lord Jesus Christ. Take a nap with Him, wake up with Him. It's a loving way to end your day – you can relax knowing He will always be with you. A personal relationship with Jesus is the best thing to ever happen to you. He has the keys to open every door. He will guard you when going out and your coming in. I am a witness that it is so.

Ask yourself, what kind of ending do you want to experience? I gave up, threw my hands up, and surrendered all – not to the police- as many of my cohorts did, but I was arrested, handcuffed, and carried away by Jesus. He spared my life, saved my soul, gave me a new beginning, and made me brand new! Yes, my scars leave me disfigured and somewhat disabled, but my disability is my strength, the beginning of getting stronger physically, mentally, and spiritually. This is a story of renewal, not an ending. It is evidence that it is not what happens to us, but how God can show up and turn our lives around. Only He knows and controls my beginning and my ending.

He will do the same for you. You can ensure that when the end comes, you will go with a peaceful smile. It is never too late to change. Take the first step towards progress – every step will get better and better. When all else has failed - try Jesus.

I like this formula by Tullian Tchividjian:

Jesus + Nothing = Everything.

CELEBRATE LIFE...CELEBRATE JESUS !!!!

"Trust in the LORD with all thine heart; And lean not unto thine own understanding. In all thy ways acknowledge him, and he shall direct thy paths."
Proverbs 3:5-6

Life Now Is Sweet, and My Joy Is Complete...

Leonard and Family

About the Author

Leonard Edward Johnson (Lenny) was born on July 26, 1957, at St. John's Episcopal Hospital in Brooklyn, New York. He was raised in the Brevoort Projects in the Bedford-Stuyvesant neighborhood of Brooklyn. Lenny married his wife Alita Norine Faircloth on September 25, 1982. Lenny has six children, Tamika, Chanelle, Gary, Malcolm, Marcus, and Crystal and five grandchildren. The family relocated to Harlem, New York in 1979. Lenny currently resides in Chesapeake, Virginia.

In 2001, Lenny gave his life to Christ – he got saved at St. Luke Baptist Church where Rev. J.G. McCann, Sr. was the pastor. On April 18, 2004, Lenny was inspired by a sermon by Rev. Al Sharpton, President of the National Action Network of which he is a member. Rev. Sharpton preached at the Ordination/Consecration service. His message was taken from Mark 11:1,4 and titled "Get Loose and Serve."

Lenny went on to serve as the armorbearer for Pastor McCann and traveled all over the country with him. During his ups and downs and numerous health challenges, in and out of the hospital, Lenny never gave up, and Pastor McCann never gave up on him. The Pastor became a trusted friend, a major inspiration in his life, and the impetus for writing this book.